Single Parenting But Not Alone

ISBN: 979-8-218-25498-8
LCCN: 2023914450

EWM Publishing
Yonkers, New York

Typeset by Michelle Cline

GEORGIANNA MARTINEZ
MOMMY

A Devotional For Moms Choosing To Do Life
With God

EVANNA MARTINEZ
DAUGHTER

You ♥ Me

This is a picture or a drawing of us

Table of Contents

Encouragement
FROM ONE SINGLE MOM TO ANOTHER

Being a single mom is not something I thought I would ever be. I grew up in a single-parent home for most of my life and I saw two of my sisters raise their children as single mothers. As a result, I was determined for that not to be my story! Yet, here I am.

The words carefully crafted and arranged will attempt to tell you that what I thought was going to be the worst situation or title bestowed upon me, on the contrary, has turned out to be the best thing that has happened to me! It is not an insignificant matter to state that being a parent is a lot of work and can be draining emotionally, physically, mentally, and even spiritually, especially if you are doing it on your own. Nevertheless, let me encourage you by telling you that with God in the equation, while in the natural realm you are physically "alone", He is right there by your side guiding you every step of the way; He collects every tear, hears every cry, feels the tiredness and pain, and responds to every prayer. Each devotional page contains space to write down declarations over your life and your prayers. Here is my declaration and prayer over you:

Prayer: I pray 2 Corinthians 9:8 over your life today. May God bless you in abundance during this season so that you may have all that you need and lack nothing. In Jesus name, Amen.
Declaration: I decree and declare that God will enlighten your mind and carry you through this journey called parenthood.

> Join me on our journey to parenting single, but not alone...

Encouragement
FROM A SINGLE MOM'S DAUGHTER

Hi! My name is Evanna, I am nine years old, and having a single mom is of no difference to me than having a dad living with me. As contradictory as this statement may be, let me explain further. I still get food, games, even toys! I don't think anything would change in my heart if I had a dad, I would love them both equally! When I think about it, I usually say, "Well, it is what it is. God will provide health and anything else we need for life." I feel completely okay without a dad. If I did have one, I would still be okay, but normalizing the absence of a father in my life was one part of the healing process.

Day 1

After my breakup, I felt all sorts of emotions: hurt, anger, brokenness, hopelessness, and the list goes on. Despite all of these emotions, I knew that I had the biggest, most fragile and valuable responsibility over me: a little person, my child. While the broken me was dominant. the level headed me, that has so much love to give, needed to win. But how? Where do I begin in order to bring her forth?. I simply needed healing. Please, do not mistake the use of the word "simply" with "lightly" or "unimportant". Rather, most times, the solution to our victory is much simpler to admit than what the storms in our lives make it seem as an impossibility to find. My soul simply needed to be mended. My heart simply needed its pieces put back together. The only way this healing process was going to take place was by simply putting my trust in God; The mender of broken hearts. I encourage you to trust Him and allow Him to be your refuge.

Prayer:

> *Lord, I come before you on this day and I present my heart to you. I ask that you be my refuge and my fortress as you mend the pieces of my heart together. I trust that you will make me whole again. Through your love I will be able to love again. In Jesus name Amen.*

Declaration:

____

____

____

____

____

____

____

Day 2

> Rejoicing in hope, patient in tribulation, continuing steadfastly in prayer.
>
> *Romans 12:12 (NKJV)*

One of the stages of healing is facing and enduring the state of feeling alone. There were many times in which I felt this way. Being in the place of loneliness comes with being accompanied by sadness, your thoughts, and eventually being led to become intimate with depression. I knew that being in this lonely place was not healthy for me or my child. The one thing I knew that was the antidote for this place was prayer. Prayer was not done as an act of ritualism, obligation, or pattern, but rather it was my desperate call for my Father. I realized that I needed to start praying again and reading the Bible during this time more than ever; the direction I needed out of the place of loneliness was through His direction alone!

Prayer:

Lord, Father God, I come before you asking you to fill this void of loneliness. Lord, I need you, I need your sweet presence. I can't do this on my own. I know that with you by my side no longer will I feel this emptiness but instead will rejoice in hope. In Jesus name Amen.

Declaration:

____

____

____

____

____

____

____

____

____

____

Day 3

> Then you shall call, and the Lord will answer; you shall cry, and He will say, 'Here I am.'
>
> Isaiah 58:9 (NKJV)

Something to remember during your time of healing is that God is omnipresent; He is everywhere at all times. You can call on Him and He will answer. Even if you think He is not there because you don't feel Him or because he has not responded, He hears you. Allow Him to wipe your tears away and soothe your soul. He is the only one who can wipe your tears, cleanse your soul, and repair your heart all at the same time!

Prayer:

Lord Father God I come before you thanking you for your omnipresence. Please help me understand what I am supposed to learn during this season in my life. I'm calling on you to wipe my tears, repair my heart, and hold me close as I cling on to you.

Declaration:

____

____

____

____

____

____

____

____

____

____

> Blessed is the man who trusts in the Lord, And whose hope is the Lord. For he shall be like a tree planted by the waters, which spreads out its roots by the river, And will not fear when heat comes; But it's leaf will be green, And will not be anxious in the year of drought, Nor will cease from yielding fruit.
>
> *Jeremiah 17:7-8 (NKJV)*

I know that at the moment it may not seem or feel like it, but you are blessed! As the scripture says, "Blessed is the man who trusts in the Lord." Although you may not see yourself or your situation as being blessed, all you have to do is trust and allow God to do the rest. Know that everything happens for a reason, it may not make sense to you now but if you stay planted or consistent in Him, as you heal, you will see the fruit of your loins at the end of this journey.

Prayer:

Lord Father God I come before you, trusting your will during this journey. Your word tells me that I am blessed as I trust and place my hope in you. As I continue to stay planted in you, please help me see the fruit in my life.

In Jesus name Amen.

Declaration:

Day 5

> I have set the Lord always before me:
> because he is at my right hand,
> I shall not be moved.
>
> Psalm 16:8 (NKJV)

As you heal, there may be times in which you may want to fill the void or hurt you are feeling. Some people do so by drinking, partying, drugs, or other countless ways. These immediate fixes that make you depend on anything other than God to get you through your healing, is only a temporary fix. After all is said and done, you are back at square one and feeling that void again; sometimes even deeper. The permanent filler of that void, which will leave you full, is Christ. I encourage you to allow him to lead you down your path of healing. The next time you feel the urge to seek fulfillment from something other than God, remember He is right by your side and nothing or no one can make you feel more complete than Him.

Prayer:

Lord, I come before you laying my hurt and my pain before you. I pray that as you sit at my right hand, you help me heal from this hurt. Father God, renew me, restore me, mend my broken pieces and make me whole.

Declaration:

Day 6

There are many levels and notions in healing. One of these aspects is understanding. As you cry out to the Lord, ask Him to help you understand what you are supposed to learn from this trial. Having an understanding of why this season had to occur would allow you to see His will for your life. Once this is done, you will get one step closer to a breakthrough in your healing process. Knowledge and wisdom allows us to not repeat the same occurrences if found in the same situation again.

Prayer:

Lord Father God I come before you asking you to illuminate my mind. Please help me make sense of this season in my life. Help me see what I am supposed to learn from this trial. Provide me with the wisdom I need to break through this portion of my journey.
In Jesus name Amen.

Declaration:

____

____

____

____

____

____

____

____

____

Day 7

There are times when hurt people tend to hurt others. As you are going through your healing season, allow God to guide you on how to approach people in different situations that arise. I remember when I had to allow God to show me how to deal with obstacles in single parenting. Especially when facing opposition from the other parent. I was able to keep a level mind by getting into God's presence daily. By praying, spending time with Him ,and meditating on His word, I was able to react with a sound mind. I encourage you to get into his presence and allow him to do the same for you.

Prayer:

Lord, I come before you asking you for strength and understanding during this trial. Please show me how to react with a sound mind. As you continue to heal me, and restore me, help me understand your ways that I may not act thoughtlessly but with love.
In Jesus name Amen.

Declaration:

Day 8

With healing comes up's and down's. There have been days when one would feel good and have the thought of, "I got this! Life is not so bad at the moment." On the other hand, there are days with moments where one can feel like a dark cloud is hanging over their head and they are in mourning. These feelings are completely okay because they are part and evidence of your healing process. What matters is not to stay in that place of hopelessness. As the verse says, "Hope in God…" during this time, it is within that hope you will find His peace. I encourage you to let out your best worship and praise to Him during your cloudy season.

Prayer:

Lord, I humbly come before you asking for your strength. My soul longs for you. With my worship I seek your face. May your presence consume me and put my soul to peace.

Declaration

EK
LOVE

EK
LOVE

Therefore I say to you,
whatever things you ask when you pray,
believe that you receive them,
and you will have them.

Mark 11:24 (NKJV)

Because of his omnipresence, we know that God hears our sorrows and prayers. As you cry out and pray to Him, do not hesitate to ask Him for what's in your heart. Although He knows our thoughts and desires, as a loving Father, He wants to hear our requests. I encourage you to ask God for whatever you need during this process of healing. Ask Him to help you understand His will for your life. With faith, as you pray, His will is fulfilled.

Prayer:

Lord Father God I come before your throne laying my partitions at your feet. God you know these days have been rough and you know what I need before I even ask. On this day I am stepping out in faith asking you to supply my needs. Your word says that I ask and it shall be received. Lord, I pray that your will be done in my life that I may receive the abundance you have for me. In Jesus name Amen.

Declaration:

____

____

____

____

____

____

____

____

Day 10

While you continue to pray and be healed during this season, keep in mind that children need to heal too. There will be times in which your child will seek the help for their healing in any place they believe can be found. Your actions during this vulnerable time can be the determining factor your child needs in their search for healing. As the verse mentions, maintain in prayer and be vigilant (paraphrased). Depending on their age, their behavior may differ. In the same way that you earnestly pray for your healing and that of your child, I encourage you to allow your child to witness your prayers; let them see. Teach them that God is the only one that can heal their hurt.

Prayer:

Lord I come before you thanking you for being my Abba, the one and only source that can heal my brokenness. As you mend my heart Lord I ask that you also remember my child(ren) during these difficult times. Like I Lord, they too need you. As we continue to cling on to you, Lord show us your Glory. In Jesus name Amen.

Declaration:

Day 11

One thing we must remember is that we are our children's first teachers. As they watch us, they learn how to navigate through life. What better way to teach them about how to get through challenging times than by being strong in God. It's okay for our children to see us cry out to God during our vulnerable moments. In this same way they will see how, after getting up, dusting our knees, and wiping our tears, we stand in the strength we receive from Him. Know that our Father's heart is for us to have life and an abundance (John 10:10 NKJV). I encourage you to stand firm in His word. Hold your head up high and continue to walk where He is leading you. As you do so, your children will watch, learn, and apply these actions during their moments of difficulty.

Prayer:

Lord, I thank you for being the rock I can stand strong in. I thank you for the courage you supply me with daily. I pray that as you are with me wherever I go, I pray that you also walk and supply my child(ren) with the same measure if not more of your courage. That during their moments of vulnerability they too remember you are with them.

Declaration:

____

____

____

____

____

____

> He has made everything beautiful
> in its time.
>
> *Ephesians 3:11 (NKJV)*

God's word says he turns beauty for ashes (Isaiah 61:3 NKJV). Although this may sound contradicting, it is saying that he has a way of turning our mess into something beautiful. As the verse states, "He already made your situation beautiful" (paraphrased). He has healed you, He has turned what you believed to be an obstacle into something that you will testify for His glory. In the spiritual realm, it has been decreed and declared, even though it may be difficult to see it during this time. As you continue to prostrate yourself at His feet and allow Him to help you carry your burdens, you will see this beauty.

Prayer:

Lord Father God as I press in to you, I pray that you can take the scales off of my eyes. I pray that today will be the day I can see what you have made beautiful. I pray that today will be the day I no longer identify with the hurt from my experience. But that I may see the beauty as I walk in your peace. In Jesus name Amen.

Declaration:

EK
LOVE

EK
LOVE

Day 13

To God be the glory, you are healed! Now what? Whether you may feel healed or think you are, it is still not 100% there. I decree and declare, you my friend, are healed in the mighty name of Jesus! I encourage you to now go deeper in Him. Seek His face, and get to know Him intimately. Allow Him to fill the void you are feeling. Shift your focus of not having a physical person with you toward having God always there. Doing this will allow you to see the promise He has for you. Think of it as seeing a rainbow after a storm.

Prayer:

Lord, I come before you and I thank you for healing my brokenness. I pray father God that you teach me how to seek you intimately. Lord, I want your ways to be my ways. Show me the way my God, as your word says I know you walk with me. In Jesus name Amen.

Declaration:

____

____

____

____

____

____

____

Day 14

> "Most assuredly, I say to you, he who believes in me, the works that I do he will do also; and greater works than these he will do, because I go to my father. And whatever you ask in my name, that I will do, that the father may be glorified in the son. If you ask anything in my name, I will do it."
>
> *John 14:12-14 (NKJV)*

What does intimacy look like? It is spending time with God in order to really get to know Him and have an understanding of Him. This special time is not a chore, obligation, or routine. True intimacy is about investing time in His presence just because you have the desire to do so; it brings you peace and excitement just thinking about it. Oftentimes we tend to get into His presence because we need something from Him. As Jesus went to His Father, let's also go to our Father (Matthew 14:23 NKJV) and spend time basking in His presence. As you read about how Jesus lived his life, whenever He was not teaching or healing, He was spending time in true intimacy with Abba.

Prayer:

Lord, Father God I come before your presence my God, I prostrate myself in spirit and truth my Lord. Show me your Glory my God. Help me seek your face, my Lord. Stir up in me the desire to seek you daily, my Lord. As your son sought you, I too Lord wish to seek more of you. In Jesus name Amen.

Declaration:

____

____

____

____

____

____

____

> "If you love me, keep my commandments.
> And I will pray the Father, and He will
> give you another Helper, that He may
> abide with you forever the Spirit of
> truth, whom the world cannot receive,
> because it neither sees Him nor knows
> Him: but you know Him for He dwells
> with you and will be in you."
>
> *John 14:15-17 (NKJV)*

True intimacy is knowing God at such a level that you know and trust what He is capable of doing in your life. Think of it as when you are in a relationship and you know each other so well that you finish each other's sentences and know what they will do in a situation because you've spent enough time with them to predict their actions and reactions. This is how close God wants to be with you, close enough that you know with certainty His capabilities in your life and situations. I encourage you to allow the Holy Spirit to dwell in you as you seek true intimacy with God.

Personal prayer:

Declaration:

____

____

____

____

____

____

____

____

____

____

> O God, you are my God; Early will I seek you; my soul thirsts for you; my flesh longs for you In a dry and thirsty land where there is no water. So I have looked for you in the sanctuary, To see your power and your Glory.
>
> *Psalm 63:1-2 (NKJV)*

While in intimacy, adorn your spirit, as you would prepare yourself for a special occasion. Think about how well your hands are manicured for this event. How you would look for the best outfit to wear or how you will make sure your hair is in perfect condition. This is how we should prepare our spirit in order to allow God to live in us. We need to prepare ourselves for Him to dwell in us. How do we do this, you may ask? First, seek him as the immediate thing to do in our day before anything else begins. As His word says, we need to thirst for Him. During this time of preparation I encourage you to ready your soul by turning on some worship music and begin to praise Him. Lay your burdens and cares to the side and free your mind. In doing so you will feel and see His Glory.

Personal prayer:

Declaration:

____

____

____

____

____

____

____

____

____

> Now a certain woman had a flow of blood for twelve years, and had suffered many things from many physicians. She had spent all that she had and was no better, but rather grew worse. When she heard about Jesus, she came behind Him in the crowd and touched His garment. For she said, "If only I may touch His clothes, I shall be made well."
>
> *Mark 5:25-28 (NKJV)*

With true intimacy, persistence and faith are needed. These two factors are what allows you to have access to God's glory. As the woman with the issue of blood, having suffered for many years knew that Jesus was the only source of healing for her recurring issue. She took advantage of the intimate moment she had with Him by getting so close to Him despite the intervening crowd. She allowed her faith to take hold of the power she knew was emanating from Him simply by touching the border of his garment. As the woman with the blood, I encourage you with faith, pursue and keep pressing into God during your intimate moments with Him. Allow His touch to make you well and restore you.

Personal prayer:

Declaration:

____

____

____

____

____

____

____

____

 Day 18

With intimacy, your faith is stretched. When things are stretched they grow. It is God's desire for His children to grow and mature in Him. It's during these intimate moments where one can be vulnerable with God. He is always ready and willing to listen to us but it is our job to seek Him. As we continue to allow ourselves to be vulnerable and lay everything down before Him, He will reveal Himself to us. Hence, our faith increases because that is the confirmation we need to continue to press on and follow him.

Personal prayer:

Declaration:

____

____

____

____

____

____

____

____

____

Day 19

> Believe me that I am in the father
> and the father in me, or else believe me
> for the sake of the works themselves.
>
> *John 14:11 (NKJV)*

As Jesus spoke to His disciples when they asked how will they know where he is going (John 14:5 NKJV), His response was that His Father was in Him because He was in His Father. When you have true intimacy with God and get to know Him more and more, you start to look like Him. As he reveals himself, He starts to reveal those things in you that do not edify Him and you. Deeper intimacy causes deeper change. Just like in a relationship, when two people are together for a long time, they start to look alike. This is what God wants for you. He wants to be so intimately close to you that He can see Himself in you and you can see yourself as He sees you.

Personal prayer:

Declaration:

Day 20

> Therefore humble yourselves under the mighty hand of God, that He may exalt you in due time, casting all your care upon Him, for He cares for you.
>
> *1 Peter 5: 6-7 (NKJV)*

Humility is needed during your intimate moments with God. Being humble is your way of telling God "here I am and I need you." God honors the humility He sees in His children. It is through this humility that he takes the load you are carrying, allowing you to rest. This humble state allows you to lower yourself so that God can elevate Himself in your life. The result of this elevation is your exaltation in God's timing.

Prayer:

Lord Father God I come before you, thanking you for this time we have together. I pray that as I continue to cast my care unto you, you continue to help me with this load. Lord as I sit at your feet, I pray that I have more of you and less of me. Please continue to guide my path as I humble myself to you.

Declaration:

____

____

____

____

____

____

____

____

____

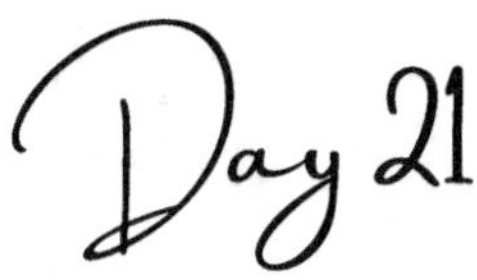

> But without faith it is impossible to please Him, for he who comes to God must believe that He is, and that He is a rewarder of those who diligently seek Him.
>
> *Hebrews 11:6 (NKJV)*

Intimacy with God requires much time and frequency in prayer. Things that have great value such as a diamond, go through a process, which requires time. The key to getting through the length of time of intimacy with God is faith. As it says in the Bible, "Faith without works is dead" (James 2:26 NKJV). In this case the "work" is carving out the time for intimacy with God. Your consistency in seeking Him will yield a great reward for you. No matter what comes your way, I encourage you to continue to persist in your intimacy with Him. Even if you can't say anything, release a cry if you have to or write to Him. Your faith is sufficient enough for Him.

Personal prayer:

Declaration:

____

____

____

____

____

____

____

____

____

> Then Samuel told him everything,
> and hid nothing from him. And he said,
> "It is the Lord. Let Him do what
> seems good to Him."
>
> 1 Samuel 3:18 (NKJV)

During intimacy, God hears your petitions. As a result, He will answer in His time. When He does, do not question or be alarmed at the answer but rather allow Him to have his way. It's important to pray for God to do His will and not ours. God designed and structured our path. He is the only one that knows the path and direction of our life. Allow Him to have total control over your life, your child's, and your home. Let go, let God, and provide Him with the opportunity to "do what seems good to Him." This is preparation for where He wants to take you. Remember, He can only move if you allow Him to; He is a gentleman. All you have to do is open your mouth and believe.

Personal prayer:

Declaration:

____

____

____

____

____

____

____

____

____

> Therefore we were buried with Him through baptism into death, that just as Christ was raised from the dead by the glory of the father, even so we also should walk in newness of life.
>
> Romans 6:4 (NKJV)

When we give God total control over our lives things start to shift. This shift first occurs on the inside. First God heals us, then He starts to expose those things in us that need to be extracted. Once He severs what no longer needs to abide in us, He begins to pour new oil into us and fill our vessels. After surrendering all, our job is to continue in intimacy with Him during this process. Intimacy equates to walking in newness, which equates to looking more like Jesus. The beauty of it all is you don't need to say anything, others will take notice, especially your children.

Prayer:

Abba as I come to you bearing and surrendering all, I pray that you take out from within me that which is not pleasing to you. Lord as you remove, I pray that you replace those things with the tools I need to not only look more like you but to be the parent you created and called me to be. May your will be done.
In Jesus name Amen.

Declaration:

Day 24

As you walk in newness and others see, so does the enemy. Trials will come but remember who changed your walk and helped you stay firm. With parenting comes all sorts of trials; there are some that can occur more than once. For example, the other parent not abiding by the agreed upon time for bringing back the child(ren) after visitation. Whatever the situation may be, I encourage you to stand firm in God. Doing so would make it less likely for your emotions to be swayed during these moments,which in turn allows your character to stay intact. The word says even the winds and the sea have to obey (Matthew 8:27 NKJV). Imagine what would happen to the situation when you do the same.

Prayer:

Lord, I come before you giving thanks for creating a newness in me. As I am in this flesh I am vulnerable to being weak. I pray that as I stand firm in you your grace fertilizes my soil so that I may continue to prosper in the way you set before me. In Jesus name Amen.

Declaration:

____

____

____

____

____

____

____

____

____

____

> I desire therefore that the men pray everywhere, lifting up holy hands, without wrath and doubting.
>
> *1 Timothy 2:8 (NKJV)*

Intimacy helps with strengthening your prayer life to combat the tricks of the enemy. This is something that I realized during the beginning stages of my single parenting season. Prayer is what carried me through the verbal abuse I experienced from my child's father. Prayer is what kept me from falling apart when I dealt with behavior issues alone. Prayer is what guided me on making decisions for the well-being of my child. One thing that is needed as you pray through your obstacles is patience and faith. Doubting tells God that you don't believe He is capable of moving that mountain in your life. If you go down that path of thinking, then why should He move it? I encourage you to continue persisting and persevering in prayer, go to God before anyone else, believe, and watch Him turn your situation around.

Personal prayer:

Declaration:

> Then Jesus said to the centurion,
> "Go your way; and as you have believed,
> so let it be done for you." And his
> servant was healed that same hour.
>
> Matthew 8:13 (NKJV)

You have to have faith that there is light at the end of this journey; Having faith and believing that God will bring you out of the season you are in, into the purpose He created you for. As the centurion knew that Jesus was the source that would solve the issue at hand (heal his sick servant) (Matthew 8:8 NKJV), we also need to remember He is the source we run to during any season of our walk. God has called us for such a time as this (Esther 4:14 NKJV). Do not dwell on your "now" but keep your faith knowing that you are connected to the source that provides the light in every circumstance.

Prayer:

Lord I come before your throne on this day not knowing what lies ahead of me but having faith in you that it is good. I pray that as I continue to walk by faith and not by sight your will can become more evident in my life. In the mighty name of Jesus Christ Amen.

Declaration:

____

____

____

____

____

____

____

____

____

> Therefore, my brethren you also have become dead to the law through the body of Christ, that you may be married to another- to Him who was raised from the dead, that we should bear fruit to God.
>
> Romans 7:4 (NKJV)

You are the shepherd God chose to raise the sheep (your kids). You bear fruit by being a good steward to what He gifted you (your kids). You can do this by speaking life into them and pouring God's love into their minds and hearts. As God makes you a new creation in Him and molds you from the inside out, He will provide you with the tools you need to be the parent He created you to be. Remember that this is a process, and not everyday is going to be a fruit-bearing day. Consider who you are married to (Him), as the verse said, "He was raised from the dead" (Romans 7:4 NKJV). As He continues to raise you up, I encourage you to remember that our jobs as parents is to bear the fruit that will ripen our child(ren) to be who He called them to be.

Prayer:

Lord as I continue to die to my flesh I pray that you provide me with the tools I need to navigate through parenthood. Being a fruit bearer that provides good ripe fruit. In Jesus name Amen.

Declaration:

Day 28

There will be moments of groaning during parenthood. The good thing is you are not parenting alone. With God, all things are possible (Matthew 19:26 NKJV) and that is what makes the load lighter to carry. He helps balance the weight. I'm sure there is a moment you can think in retrospect and realize how God's hand was intertwined in the situation. Now, imagine how that same moment would have turned out had He not been in your life. If you are currently going through a difficult situation in your parenting journey, I encourage you to think about the last time God made a way when you thought there was no way. Continue to walk alongside Him down the narrow path as your victory is waiting for you on the other side of the gate.

Personal prayer:

Declaration:

> Remember the things I have done in the past. For I alone am God! I am God, and there is none like me. Only I can tell you the future before it even happens. Everything I plan will come to pass, for I do whatever I wish.
>
> *Isaiah 46:9-10 (NLT)*

During difficult periods in my parenting journey, I remember feeling like I was being punished because I had my child out of wedlock. I would say to myself, "This is all my fault. I wouldn't be going through this if I would have made better decisions". But even through the messes we tend to put ourselves through, God swoops in and becomes the Savior that He is. Today I encourage you to remember, recognize, and realize that there are no mistakes with God. He knew that you would be at this place at this very moment. As it says in the verse, "He alone is God…" (Isaiah 46:9 NLT) and is the only one that knows your future because He created it. I encourage you to get into your secret place and ask Him to reveal to you what you have been asking for; even if it is just a glimpse. Remember the God we serve never leaves us!

Personal prayer:

Declaration:

____

____

____

____

____

____

____

____

____

> The Lord says, "I will rescue those who love me. I will protect those who trust in my name. When they call on me, I will answer; I will be with them in trouble. I will rescue and honor them."
>
> *Psalms 91:14-15 (NLT)*

In moments where you need to make decisions and feel alone, trust that He is with you. As the verse above states, He is the protector of those who trust in Him. As you do your part in securing and continuing a relationship with Him, He will answer your call. In fact, He is already answering as He works within and molds you. He is with and has restored you. Because of this restoration, trust yourself during decision-making moments for your child(ren). Your faith gives you the strength to call on Him; He will honor it and show you the right way to go. I encourage you to present anything and everything before Him. Then, watch how secure you will feel when it's time to make a decision.

Prayer:

Lord, I come before you because you know all of the answers. You knew I was coming before this situation even occurred. As your word instructs me to ask, I come to you asking for direction in this situation. Lord your ways are the best ways and I trust that you will lead me to deciding what is best in this situation. In Jesus name Amen.

Declaration:

____

____

____

____

____

____

____

Day 31

When raising children with God by your side you have an advantage because the Holy Spirit within provides you with the tools for trying times. There was a moment in which my daughter was pulling out her hair. This was devastating to me because she would not provide me with an answer as to why this was occurring. She would instead ask me to pray and ask God why it was happening. As I prayed about it, the Holy Spirit revealed to me the need to pray targeted prayers because there was some spiritual warfare going on in the situation. Along with targeted prayers, the Holy Spirit led me to go over affirmations with her daily. After doing both things, I saw a change within my daughter. She walked around with so much confidence and assurance of being the child of God He created her to be. I encourage you to stay alert, being sober and vigilant at all times.

Personal prayer:

Declaration:

____

____

____

____

____

____

Day 32

Another benefit of raising children with God by your side as well as having God in your life, generally speaking, is the advantage of prayer. This is an advantage because it's something that is readily available and is always heard. It does not cost you anything. When we pray, God inclines His ear and the Holy Spirit delivers the message answering our call. When you need strength to get through your day because the kids are driving you crazy or work is too much to handle, when opposition comes, and/or when the enemy throws his darts, remember to call upon the Lord and don't forget to listen for his response because He always answers.

Personal prayer:

Declaration:

____

____

____

____

____

____

____

____

____

EK

LOVE

EK

LOVE

Day 33

> And He said to me, "My grace is sufficient for you, for my strength is made perfect in weakness."
>
> *2 Corinthians 12:9 (NKJV)*

During life and especially during parenting, there are many moments of weakness. You may want to give up because you are tired. Tired of repeating yourself, tired of yelling, or tired of having to stay up until your child falls asleep at night. As a single parent, especially the custodial parent, the bulk of the child rearing falls on you. As a result there is added pressure, whatever may be the reason for you wanting to give up, know that He is with you even if you don't feel it. As the verse states, "His grace is sufficient enough..." (2 Corinthians 12:9 NKJV) to get you through any obstacle that comes at you. I encourage you today to pray and ask your Abba for the strength you need that will carry you through this moment of weakness.

Personal prayer:

Declaration:

____

____

____

____

____

____

____

____

____

Day 34

> That the sharing of your faith
> may become effective by the
> acknowledgment of every good thing
> which is in you in Christ Jesus.
>
> *Philemon 1:6 (NKJV)*

Your children need a foundation in God. With this foundation the generational curses break and do not carry on into their lives. With a foundation in God, you teach your children who they should run to in times of need. You are their initial access to God. I encourage you to allow them to see you go to God's feet during your trying moments. Children learn and do what they see and not by what we tell them. Whenever your child is expressing his/her difficult moment, bring them into your prayer closet and guide them on how to pray the targeted prayers that will help them overcome the adversary in their lives.

Prayer:

Lord Father God I come before you knowing that you hold the answer to all things. Your word says that all I need is faith the size of a mustard seed. Today I use that faith and ask that you guide me by providing me with the tools and understanding to teach my child your ways. Lord help me show how just by having a mustard seed of faith is all it takes for you to move in any situation. In Jesus name Amen.

Declaration:

Day 35

Our children learn not by what we tell them but by what they see us do and say. Let's be slow to anger so that our children can grow with healthy emotions,as we continue to draw nearer to God, as He continues to mold us. Allow God to show us how to teach them and how to cultivate their emotions to express themselves. Today, I encourage you to speak with your child about the situation at hand, whatever it may be. Show him/her how to pray for forgiveness. Doing so will teach them how to go to the Father after a mistake is made.

Prayer:

Lord, I come before you and I repent for all of the things I have done and said that were not pleasing to you. Please forgive me for acting in ways that you did not intend for me to react. Father may you deliver me from any anger, resentment, and any other feelings that causes me to not reflect you. As you cleanse me and deliver me, Father I ask that you restore what was broken and fill me up with more of you. In Jesus name Amen.

Declaration:

Day 36

living in a world filled with darkness, but having the source of light guiding us through life and parenting, allows us to know and recognize what true love really is. This is because God IS love. The result of having God's love is that we have the opportunity to raise our children in it; in Him. As he or she grows in love, it will develop and cultivate. This leads to love being secured within them and not depart from them. Through this love God will abide and His light will continue to shine through, within, and around them. This sets the framework that everything he/she does will be done with and out of the love of God.

Prayer:

Lord I come before you thanking you for your Agape, your love that surpasses all understanding. I pray that you teach me how to love as you love. Help me see people as you see them so that I can love my neighbor as myself. It is through this love that I can set the foundation for my children to understand and learn of your love. In Jesus name Amen.

Declaration:

____

____

____

____

____

____

____

____

____

Day 37

As Hannah was aware, we too need to realize that children are gifts from God and they are not permanently ours. We have to do our part while we have them by cherishing and caring for them as they are not only precious to us but to the Lord as well. One thing we need to remember is that our shepherding (raising) changes throughout the different seasons (ages) of our children. Therefore, our cultivation and teaching should look different according to age. How we raise our children at the age of eight looks different when they are thirteen. I encourage you to ask the Lord to provide you with the insight on how to raise your child(ren) according to the season they are in and to provide you with the understanding to meet their needs throughout every season of their lives.

Personal prayer:

Declaration:

____

____

____

____

____

____

____

____

____

Day 38

> Now when she had weaned him, she took him up with her, with three bulls, one ephah of flour, and a skin of wine, and brought him to the house of the Lord in Shiloh. And the child was young.
>
> 1 Samuel 1:24 (NKJV)

Our role as parents is to raise our children with God guiding us. When our children enter an age in which they start to manage their own life, their decisions are theirs, as long as you do your part, God does the rest. Our part is setting the foundation in God; teaching them how to go to God in prayer for all things and providing the room for understanding things of the world so that they can see the goodness of having God in their life. Doing so will help them distinguish and determine the best path to walk in life.

Prayer:

Lord Father God I come before you thanking you for the gift that is my child. Lord as you called me to be the shepherd that instructs my child in the way that they should go. I ask for the understanding, knowledge, and tools that I need to show them your ways that they may remember and not depart from it. In Jesus name Amen.

Declaration:

____

____

____

____

____

____

____

____

____

Day 39

A benefit that our children will receive for having a foundation in God is mercy. Mercy is the compassion or forgiveness shown toward someone whom it is within one's power to punish or harm. God being a God of love seeks only goodness for his children. Because we have this flesh and live in human form, we need his grace and mercy daily. It is through this grace and mercy that we can live and survive in this world. Fear of the Lord produces His mercy. The core component in a foundation of living in Christ is understanding that living in fear of the Lord is being in obedience to Him. When we live in obedience our children will see it and learn how to live in obedience as well.

Prayer:

Lord, I come before you, thanking you for your grace and mercy. I pray that as the day is new you pour out a fresh new anointing into this vessel. Lord give me the strength and understanding of how to live in obedience to your word. That my children may see and live in obedience to you as well. In Jesus name Amen.

Declaration:

____

____

____

____

____

____

Day 40

The term fear of God is equivalent to living your life in obedience. God calls us to be the light and show love in this world. We can do this by exhibiting Godly characteristics: love, joy, peace, longsuffering, kindness, goodness, faithfulness, gentleness, and self-control. Because our children learn by example, it is important that we show these characteristics during trying times. When they see obedience in action, they will be able to identify the moments in which one is not living in obedience. A teachable moment I've lived was through moments of road rage. There were times where I would get upset while driving and would verbalize my frustration. During those times my daughter would remind me to have self-control by asking me to breathe and calm down. I encourage you to continue living in obedience so that your children may continue to see it and not only apply it to your life when needed but theirs as well.

Personal prayer:

Declaration:

____

____

____

____

____

____

____

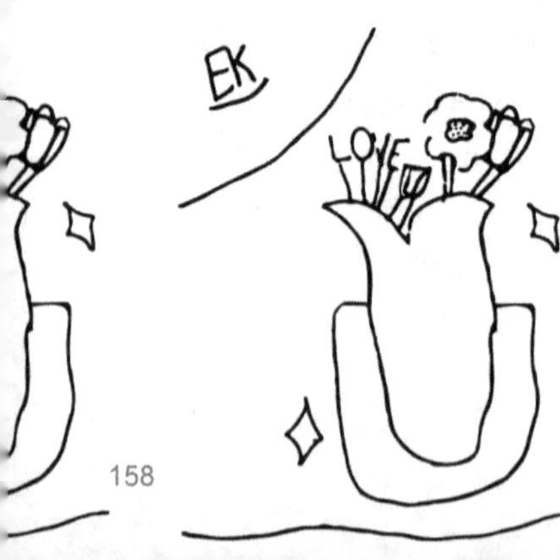

EK
LOVE

EK
LOVE

> In the fear of the Lord there is strong confidence, And His children will have a place of refuge.
>
> *Proverbs 14:26 (NKJV)*

When children walk in fear of the Lord they will have confidence in their walk with Him, especially when they are out in the world. They will be secure in their walk because they will see the proof in our lives as their parents and at home. Although walking in fear of the Lord is a concept that is general across all ages, it looks different according to age. A child being obedient at the age of seven can look different compared to a child who is seventeen. One thing that I've learned to do, and I encourage you to do, is acknowledge and show appreciation to your children when you hear that he/she has done something positive or kept in obedience when you were not around. For example, when I told my daughter not to run in the church, a member from the church came to me and told me how my daughter told one of her friends that she could not run because her mother told her not to and she advised her friend not to as well. When I spoke to my daughter about it she was happy to hear my words and brought into remembrance something I always told her, which was that God sees everything. Acknowledging His omnipresence births obedience, which in turn brings forth the confidence in their walk.

Personal prayer:

Declaration:

____

____

____

____

____

____

____

____

____

____

____

____

____

____

____

____

____

Day 42

As Jesus acknowledges in this verse, He alone can do nothing without the Father. As parents, we too need this understanding. We need to realize and remember that our children learn from us. For this reason, we need to be careful with everything that we do, in all that they see, and feel. Hence, it is why we need to allow God to show us the things from our past and upbringing that we need to break from and prevent from projecting to our children. One thing the love of God has shown me in my walk is the lack of loving affection I received from my mom. I rarely heard her tell me that she loved me. After this revelation, I made a choice to change the trajectory and how I project love towards my daughter. Not only do I remind her of how much I love her repeatedly but I also make it a habit to hug her many times throughout the day. I allow her to feel loved and remind her that God's love is the best love anyone can ever receive. Today, I encourage you to ask the Lord to reveal to you the things that need to be fixed and discarded so that the chains can break and change you and your family's trajectory.

Personal prayer:

Declaration:

____

____

____

____

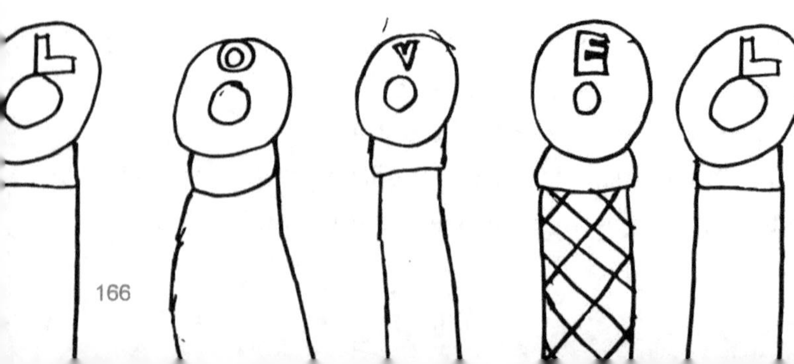

Day 43

Our children learn about authority from us. Learning how to obey from an early age will help them have the understanding and practice of obedience to God, whom is authority. Reacting or responding impulsively is an element that can come up when responding to authority. There can be times when one would choose not to do something because they are upset or feel emotional about something. When dealing with authority, we need to think and act despite how we feel. One way to guide our children is by emphasizing the fact that although they may not want to do something, like going to school, it's something that needs to be done because it prepares them for the working world. Another way to teach our children about authority is by reminding them that respecting authority here on Earth is also honoring God; He placed those people in those authoritative positions.

Prayer:

Lord Father God I come before you, asking for strength. My child looks to me as an example. I pray that he/she can see my obedience to you so they may grow in obedience to your authority. In Jesus name Amen.

Declaration:

____

____

____

____

____

____

____

Day 44

> My son, hear the instruction of
> your father, And do not forsake the
> law of your mother; for they will be a
> graceful ornament on your head,
> And chains about your neck.
>
> Proverbs 1:8-9 (NKJV)

As the shepherds we are to our children, we have a responsibility to teach them to hear God, the filler of the void of their earthly father. As we teach, God will also instruct through us; He is the one who provides us with the tools for the instruction. As parents we need to make sure that our teachings are aligned with living a Godly lifestyle, which requires obedience. By being watchful of what our children are watching, hearing, and entertaining, we are able to accomplish this. There are some things, with conviction from the Holy Spirit, that we must be sensitive to changing in our lives. Music is a component which we should be aware of. God created us to worship Him, as our children see us worship, they will follow suit. Music has a way of tugging on one's emotions, which is the reason why it is more beneficial to listen to worship music as opposed to worldly music because it is edifying.

Personal prayer:

Declaration:

Day 45

A part of living a life in obedience to God is the awareness our children need in honoring both parents. Although the other parent is not present, it's our job to remind our children during needed moments to honor and respect that parent. Oftentimes, it can be hard to show support for someone who has wronged you. I'm sure there have been thoughts of, "I do all of the work of raising, he does not deserve their honor." Nevertheless, God wants us to remember that we are to be a reflection of Him. As Christ forgives, we also must and will begin to look at and love others as Christ does. Doing so shows how we are obedient in our walk, which in turn will allow us to be a living example of obedience for our children.

Prayer:

Lord Father God I humbly come before you thanking you for the opportunity to be an example of obedience for my child. I pray that you search my heart and take out what is not of you that I may continue to have a pure heart to love as you love. In Jesus name, Amen.

Declaration:

____

____

____

____

____

____

____

____

____

Day 46

> Let us therefore come boldly
> to the throne of grace, that we
> may obtain mercy and find grace
> to help in time of need.
>
> *Hebrews 4:16 (NKJV)*

If you are feeling frustrated about something or your child has done something to anger you, go before God and ask for guidance on how to handle the situation. Do not be rash in disciplining your child out of frustration. God is available to lead you through this. His grace is sufficient enough to get you through any obstacle you face. Allow His grace to be the rock in which you draw your strength from. I encourage you to lean into His grace, let Him embrace you, and hear the instruction He is giving you on how to respond to the matter at hand.

Personal prayer:

Declaration:

____

____

____

____

____

____

____

____

> Discipline your children, and they
> will give you peace; they will bring
> you the delights you desire.
>
> *Proverbs 29:17 NIV*

Although everyone has their own belief and way of disciplining their children, disciplining my child is something that I really struggled with and prayed to God for direction about. There is one thing that God made clear to me and that is to discipline with love. As God calls us to do everything through Christ's love, disciplining is also one of those things. In the book of Genesis, God gives instruction to man (Adam) and woman (Eve) on how to move forward in their roles in the home. For Eve, it was to take care and nurture. In order to nurture, love is needed. I encourage you today as the sole disciplinarian in your home to allow God's grace to guide you during moments of discipline and let His grace be the love you show your child.

Prayer:

Lord, I come before you, thanking you for your grace. This grace that is sufficient enough to get me through any obstacle I encounter. I pray that your grace strengthens me and teaches me how to discipline my child with love and not wrath. In Jesus's name, Amen.

Declaration:

Day 48

> A soft answer turns away wrath,
> But a harsh word stirs up anger.
>
> *Proverbs 15:1 (NKJV)*

Discipling with love is having the understanding that yelling at children does more harm than good. As the verse above dictates, yelling causes more frustration and adds more "fuel to the fire". If a child does something that requires a response of discipline, take a moment, pray, and collect your thoughts before responding. Allow God to instruct you on how to respond in a loving and healthy way. Naturally, because we are human, there may be times in which anger may stir. If this ever happens, God will be waiting with open arms, seek his forgiveness, and make things right with your child. There is nothing wrong with apologizing to our children, seeing this humility will help them as well. Disciplining with love helps raise children that do not have to heal from their childhood when they grow older.

Personal prayer:

Declaration:

____

____

____

____

____

____

____

____

____

EK
EK
LOVE
LOVE

> Love suffers long and is kind; love does not envy; love does not parade itself, is not puffed up; does not behave rudely, does not seek its own, is not provoked, thinks no evil, does not rejoice in iniquity, but rejoices in the truth; bears all things, believes all things, hopes all things, endures all things.
>
> *1 Corinthians 13:4-7 (NKJV)*

Longsuffering is something that single parents endure. The term longsuffering means "to have or show patience during times of trouble" (Oxford Languages). It's an active response to opposition; not surrendering or giving up because of obstacles. The only way to get through longsuffering is with the love and the peace of God; a peace that surpasses all understanding (Philipians 4:7 NKJV). Having the love of Christ for others helps you see others as Christ sees them. I encourage you to replace your name wherever you see the word love in the verse above. Doing so during difficult moments can bring you the peace you need to push through and persevere during adversaries.

Prayer:

Lord Father God I come before you during this moment in my life where the pressure is thickening and coming from all places. Lord, I pray that you can help me love others as you love. Help me see as you do that I may have your peace in the midst of this storm.
In Jesus name Amen.

Declaration:

____

____

____

____

____

____

____

E
W
M

> But the fruit of the spirit is love, joy, peace, longsuffering, kindness, goodness, faithfulness, gentleness, self-control. Against such there is no law.
>
> *Galatians 5:22-23 (NKJV)*

Along with being an attribute that has to be endured during the season of single parenting, longsuffering is a fruit of the Spirit. Therefore, it's important that our children witness our endurance with God as our rock and strength. Children learn most by what they see compared to what they hear. If they see their mothers go to God to draw strength during longsuffering or if they see their mom react to adversaries with love and peace, they, too, will learn how to endure longsuffering in their seasons of difficulties. Exhibiting the fruits of the Spirit is a way for people to see Christ in us. As our children see Christ in us, they will be able to follow suit and reflect the same, causing our children to change the trajectory of their lives as well as those around them.

Personal prayer:

Declaration:

____

____

____

____

____

____

____

____

____

Day 51

Going out as a single parent with your children can feel like one of the toughest things to do because when going out, let's say to the zoo or amusement parks, what we usually see are families with both parents. As a single parent this can be hard to look at or make you feel as if your family is incomplete. I encourage you to, like Moses when he was leading the people of Israel to the promised land and asked God to be with them on their journey, ask God to do the same. God's presence is available at any time and place, you don't have to feel alone in a place where you see other families. God's grace is sufficient enough to give you the strength to enjoy your time with your children anywhere you go. All that is required of you is to invite Him and let Him dwell in and around you. Once you do so, as Exodus 33 states, "His presence will be with you and give you rest" (v.13, NIV).

Personal prayer:

Declaration:

Day 52

As you rest in God and allow Him to be your comfort, your children will also benefit from it. These are the moments where we can take the opportunity to speak with our children and remind them of God's covering. Pray with them and together ask God to continue being the comforter that fills the void of a father-figure being in the home. Doing so would not only bring comfort and strength to your child, but will also give you the wisdom on how to support your child during these moments.

Prayer:

Lord Father God I come before you thanking you for the comfort and strength you provide to me during the season in my life. Lord, I need your help, guide me on how to comfort my child during this season. Teach me how to show them that your grace is sufficient enough for our family during this time. As you comfort me, I pray my child feels your embrace as well. In Jesus name Amen.

Declaration:

____

____

____

____

____

____

____

____

____

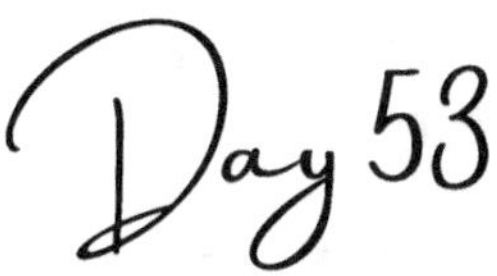

> "For the Holy Spirit will teach you in that very hour what you ought to say."
>
> *Luke 12:12 (NKJV)*

Statistics state that children who are raised in single parent homes will become single parents as well *(https://ifstudies. org/blog/disentangling-the-effects-of-family-structure-on-boys-and-girls).* I am a part of this statistic, but my daughter will have a different story. I can confidently decree and declare that she will not continue the cycle of single parenthood because God orders my steps and the Holy Spirit teaches me how to be the mother God created me to be, in His image. When we allow the Holy Spirit to be our teacher, He shifts the thinking we acquired from our upbringing and culture. For example, growing up in a single parent home often lead to emotional neglect. My mother rarely hugged me or told me that she loved me. I could have continued this very treatment with my daughter. On the other hand, with the love of God over my life, the Holy Spirit teaches me how to raise my daughter with this very love. On this day, I encourage you to ask the Holy Spirit to be your teacher. Think about the areas in your parenting you need help in. Confess them unto the Lord and watch him send the Helper that gets the job done.

Personal prayer:

Declaration:

____

____

____

____

____

____

____

Day 54

> So God created man in His own image;
> in the image of God He created him;
> male and female He created them. Then
> God blessed them, and God said to them,
> "Be fruitful and multiply; fill the Earth
> and subdue it; have dominion over the
> fish of the sea, over the birds of the
> aire, and over every living thing that
> moves on the Earth."
>
> *Genesis 1:27-28 (NKJV)*

When God created Adam and Eve he did so placing a purpose in each of them both separately and together. Together, their general purpose was to be "fruitful and multiply" (Genesis 1:28 NKJV). In order for its fulfillment, Adam and Eve need to understand and surrender to their individual purposes. Just because there is no Adam in your home, it does not mean that your home cannot be fruitful! Your relationship with God will determine its fruitfulness. The more you get closer to Him and lean in to hear His instruction on how to take care of your home, the more you will know how to provide the tenderness and care your home and children need in order to be healthy and fruitful in their own lives.

Prayer:

Lord Father God I come before you thanking you for making me in your image. I thank you for the strength and guidance you have and continue to provide me during this season in my life. Lord, I pray for more instruction and direction from you, be the Adam that my home lacks and give me the strength to continue doing my part so that my home and family may continue to bear fruit. In Jesus name Amen.

Declaration:

____

____

____

____

____

____

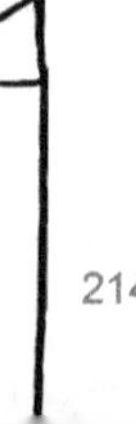
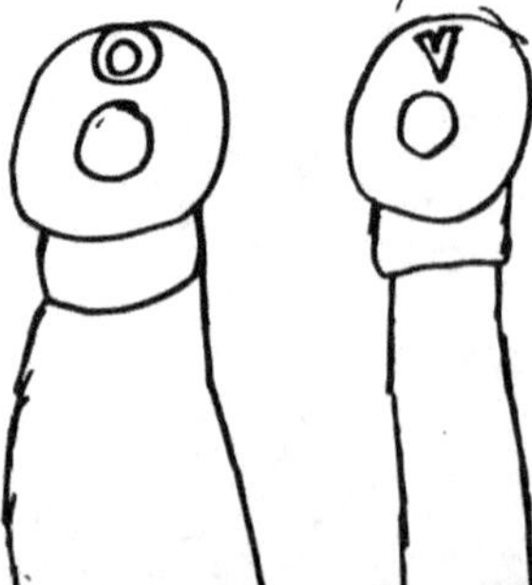

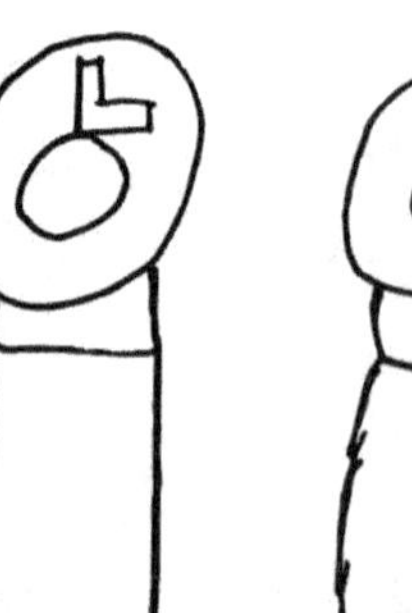

Day 55

> "I will be father to you, And you
> shall be my sons and daughters,
> says the Lord Almighty."
>
> *2 Corinthians 6:18 (NKJV)*

Although there is no physical father-figure in the home, children need to know and gain an understanding of the importance of a father in their lives. There are things that as mothers we will not be able to help our children with. We need to remember the purpose God created us for when speaking about our position in a family. As mothers (woman) we are to love and nurture our children. Despite our feelings about the father of our children, it's our duty to make sure our children know that a father is needed and has a role to fulfill in their lives as well. Having this understanding will show our children, particularly our girls in this context, the importance of a male-covering when she has her family. For our boys, the importance of a father's role will help them be the father God created them to be. Today, I want to encourage you, as God is your strength and source of direction through this season of life, to be the teacher your children need. Show them how to allow God to be the father-figure they need to teach them what they are not receiving from their earthly father.

Personal prayer:

Declaration:

____

____

____

____

____

____

____

____

> For we are His workmanship,
> created in Christ Jesus for good works,
> which God prepared beforehand that
> we should walk in them.
>
> *Ephesians 2:10 (NKJV)*

Despite the season(s) or the circumstance(s) we are facing, one thing that is important to remember is that our identity is not what society labels us as "single mothers". The verse above reminds us that we are God's workmanship; we are His "masterpiece", "His work of art", created for good works. In order to create a masterpiece, time is needed. Once the masterpiece is complete, its beauty and uniqueness is uncanny; only one of a kind. That is how God created us to be. As we embrace being His created masterpiece, it is of the essence to show our children that they too are unlike anyone else in this life; God created only one of them. In a world where there are so many labels, options, and overall confusion, it's important that we remind our children that God makes no mistakes when creating His masterpiece; He is intentional and purpose-driven. In turn, our children stay grounded in their belief of who God created them to be.

Prayer:

Lord Father God I come before you and I thank you for creating me as the unique masterpiece I am. Lord, I come before you lifting my child up as there is so much confusion going on in this world. I pray that the identity you've given to my child can be recognized, embraced, and that he/she may be grounded in being the masterpiece you created them to be. In Jesus name Amen.

Declaration:

____

____

____

____

____

____

Day 57

There are times where single parenting calls for the opportunity of co-parenting. This is depending on the circumstance and the relationship with the other parent. With co-parenting comes varying aspects, like making important decisions for the child. Through these decision-making moments, there may be times where disagreements will arise. These are moments in which we need to go to God for guidance. The word tells us that there is power in the tongue; the power of life and death (Proverbs 18:21 NKJV). God wants us to go to Him before responding during an argument. As the verse above says, "Teach me, and I will hold my tongue" (v.24 NKJV). God will provide the right words for the response needed at the perfect time: A response that will be reflective of His light in your life. Today, I encourage you to run to our "...good good..." (Good Good Father by Chris Tomlin) Father and ask Him to teach you the best way to respond to your vicissitude.

Personal prayer:

Declaration:

____

____

____

____

____

____

____

____

> But the Lord has been my defense,
> And my God the rock of my refuge.
> He has brought on them their own
> inquiry. And shall cut them off in their
> own wickedness; The Lord our God
> shall cut them off.
>
> *Psalm 94:22-23 (NKJV)*

All in all, God is our defender! Allow Him to fight your battles, whether it be as an adversary that comes through the other parent or a nagging situation with your child/children, present the situation to God. He is our rock in which we can lean on and gain our strength from (Psalm 18:2 NKJV). In all matters of life, God wants us to go to Him but there are certain situations in which He wants us to let go and let Him handle it. Our job is to surrender it all to Him and continue to pray in faith until it is all done. Allow God to deal with the person. The situation may be difficult, hurtful, maybe even unbearable, but remember the fight is not with flesh and blood but with the spirit (Ephesians 6:12 NKJV). Today I encourage you to get into your prayer closet and surrender it all to Him.

Personal prayer:

Declaration:

____

____

____

____

____

____

____

____

____

Day 59

With the load carried during single parenting, there can be moments of anxiety. When one thinks about all of the tasks that have to be fulfilled, in what may seem like such little time, there is a sense of pressure that arises. There is a key word in the verse above that speaks volumes about these moments, the word "within" (v.19). When we keep things within they tend to fester and grow. What grows is not fruitful because the product of it is "anxiety". During these moments it is important that we go to God, our comforter and soother of our soul. God does not want us to live a life full of anxiety and panic because both do not emanate from Him. Today, I encourage you to release the anxiety that stirs up in the midst of pressure. Release it to the one and only true source that depressurizes you and brings comfort and peace.

Prayer:

Lord, Father, God I come before you thanking you for another day of life. I thank you for what you have brought me out of and where you currently placed me. Lord, I present any anxiety, discord, and discomfort that is attempting to arise in me. May your comfort and peace bring stability to my mind and emotions. In Jesus's name, Amen.

Declaration:

Day 60

> For whatever is born of God overcomes the world. And this is the victory that has overcome the world-our faith.
>
> *1 John 5:4 (NKJV)*

Being born of God is trusting in Him and the word He has spoken over your life and of your children. When we trust in God we become victorious. Not only do we overcome the world but the obstacles that come with it: Through our faith. Faith is believing in what is not seen. There may be a mess in your world right now, the kids not listening, a bill not being paid, or feeling like there is not enough time in a day to get things done. Whatever the obstacle/challenge in your life, know that because of your trust in God, you already have the victory! Today, I encourage you to continue to go forth in faith. As all things occur in the spirit before it reaches the natural, you may not see the victory, but it is established. God did not bring you this far to leave you defeated.

Personal prayer:

Declaration:

Day 61

In the same way it is our responsibility to teach our children how to walk, talk, and eat with utensils, it's our charge to disciple our children and teach them the importance of living life with God in the center. Feeding and nurturing their "spirit man" is just as important for survival as nurturing their physical and emotional being. Teaching children has different aspects, such as reading and studying the word with them. It is through love that discipline and correction will help them be able to understand the importance of adhering to authority. As they grow older, this respect of authority will transfer to obeying God as authority in their lives when they are no longer in the care of a parent. I encourage you to go to God and ask Him to provide you with the strategy for the best way to disciple your children.

Personal prayer:

Declaration:

Day 62

Another form of discipleship or feeding your child's "spirit man" is by cultivating the gifts God has planted in them. In order to do so, we need to be vigilant. What does this look like? Spending time with our children and being intentional about understanding what their interests and talents are. An example of this is by noticing that your child loves to sing and can hold a note. As parents, we have the ability to go to God and ask Him for revelation and confirmation about singing being a gift He has deposited in them. Once a gift is noticed, we are not the only ones who notice as well, the devil is everwatchful. Moreover, we need to be watchful of our children, making sure that through cultivation our children are using their gifts and talents for the kingdom of God. I encourage you today to continue being the food source that feeds your child's soul.

Prayer:

Lord, I come before you thanking you for the seed you've planted in my child. I ask that you reveal and confirm the gifts you have deposited in my child. May you provide me with the tools I need to protect and cultivate the seed you have planted in your creation.

Declaration:

____

____

____

____

____

____

____

____

> "What man of you, having a
> hundred sheep, if he loses one of them,
> does not leave the ninety-nine in the
> wilderness, and go after the one which
> is lost until he finds it?"
>
> *Luke 15:4 (NKJV)*

Jesus, in the parable above, is using the sheep analogy to show how he cares for lost souls. He would leave many to go find that one that is lost and in need of Abba Father. Hence, when we pray to Him he inclines His ear. The same way God is readily available for us, we need to be readily available in the lives of our children. God is able to answer when we call on Him because He is present in our lives. We too need to be present in our children's lives. Being present is the only way we will know what their needs are. In this world where there's non-stop movement and responsibilities, I encourage you to be intentional about spending that quality time with your child. Even if it's just for 20 minutes out of the day, it will feel like eternity for them. Think about how you feel when your Abba Father leaves the 99 for you.

Personal prayer:

Declaration:

Day 64

> And whatever you do , do it heartily,
> as to the Lord and not to men, knowing
> that from the Lord you will receive
> the reward of the inheritance;
> for you serve the Lord Christ.
>
> *Colossians 3:23-24 (NKJV)*

There are moments in single parenting where there is so much taking place all at once and we begin to feel overwhelmed. Handling situations with children, alone, can feel burdensome. During these moments we need to remember God's word; whether a word was prophetically spoken over your life or there was a verse in the Bible that resonated with you and is implanted in your heart. God's word is the same yesterday, today, and forever. His words and faithfulness will be the key to lightening the overwhelming feeling. When we accomplish duties as a single mother, we need to remember to do so on to the Lord, in worship to Him. Today, I encourage you to remember that raising children is an act of service to God. Because you are serving Him, it will feel less overwhelming.

Personal prayer:

Declaration:

> And He said to them "come aside by yourselves to a deserted place and rest a while." For there were many coming and going, and they did not even have time to eat.
>
> *Mark 6:31 (NKJV)*

With single parenting comes a lot of responsibilities and long schedules. There can be moments where we can put our children and their needs before ours. This is not healthy or how God intends for us to live. God even took a day of rest after creating Earth (Genesis 2:2 NKJV). The only way, we as custodial parents ,can be the best we can be for our children is by getting the replenishment we need to keep going. It's okay to unplug from being "mommy", the verse above says so. Today, I encourage you to take some time and do something for you: unplug! Think about what would help recharge your battery. Do that very thing and rest in God as you do. It will not only benefit you but your children as well.

Prayer:

Lord, I come before you thanking you for sustaining me through life. I pray that as I rest in you, you fill my cup. Lord restore me, may your grace and mercy overflow my cup. That it may spill over onto my children. In Jesus name Amen.

Declaration:

____

____

____

____

____

____

____

____

Day 66

Although seasons change (children age) during parenting, what remains the same is God's grace that sustains you. Don't let what your eyes see deter, nor discourage or distract you from believing the promises God has spoken over your life and that of your children. Yes, there will be moments where you feel like you don't even recognize the human being you birthed and raised anymore. This can happen especially during teenage years. Today I encourage you to run to the Father, who is your safe haven. These are the times when we need to spend that overtime on our knees in that prayer closet. Remember to stay rooted and anchored to Him during all seasons of parenting because as the verse states, "...the Lord is a strong tower" (v.10) .Allow Him to be the source of your strength.

Personal prayer:

Declaration:

____

____

____

____

____

____

____

____

____

> A man who has friends must himself
> be friendly, But there is a friend
> who sticks closer than a brother.
>
> Proverbs 18:24 (NKJV)

Being a single mom can sometimes mean having a busy schedule. As a result, decisions on how time is spent have to be prioritized. Sometimes, this can lead to not having time to spend with friends or speak to them frequently on the phone. This can lead to feeling like you can't relate to certain friends you encounter in life, especially if they do not have kids or a similar experience as yours. I want to encourage you to remember God is a friend that will always be there for you and understand you. As the verse reminds us, He "...sticks closer than a brother" (v.24). Although He will never leave you, I encourage you to ask Him to send the right people that will support you and stick with you. God's intention is for His children not to go through life alone.

Personal prayer:

Declarations:

> Wisdom and knowledge will be the
> stability of your times. And the
> strength of salvation; The fear
> of the Lord is His treasure.
>
> *Isaiah 33:6 (NKJV)*

One of the many names God is referred to is "Jehovah Jireh", which translates to provider (Genesis 22:14 KJV). As single mothers, His provision increases and is evident. God provides for single parent homes in many ways; financially, spiritually, physically, and emotionally. Wisdom and knowledge, two aspects that are needed when raising children single but not alone, are a part of God's provision. As the verse states, balance is established when "...wisdom and knowledge..." (v.6) are present. These two aspects are needed to make decisions in the home and maintain its stability. When we rely on God, He provides us with the wisdom and knowledge we need to navigate through our daily lives. Today, I encourage you to take some time with Jireh, your provider, and ask Him to fill you with the wisdom and knowledge you need for your current season.

Personal prayer:

Declaration:

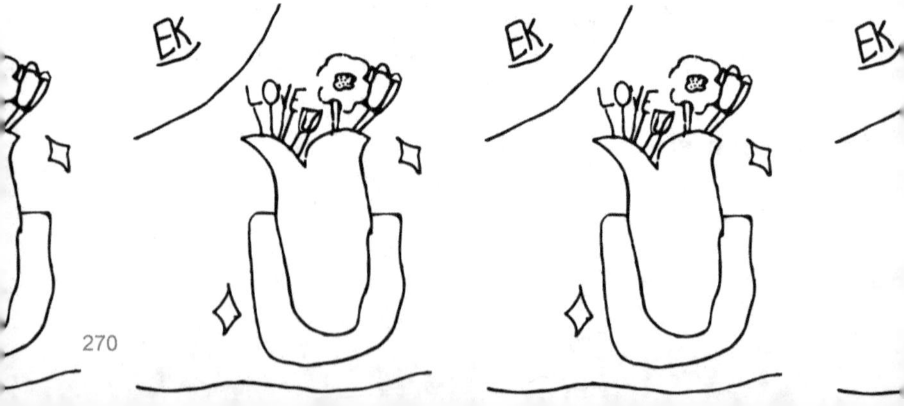

____

____

____

____

____

____

____

____

____

Day 69

> For His anger is but for a moment, His favor is for life; weeping may endure for a night, But joy comes in the morning.
>
> Psalm 30:5 (NKJV)

As the seasons of the weather change, the seasons in our lives change. It's important to remember this fact during your single mommy season. As the verse dictates, after weeping what follows is joy (v.5). God has an expiration date for every season He allows in our lives. What's important is that we don't stay in a season longer than we are supposed to. The only way to break out of seasons that are past due their expiration date is to allow God to renew our minds daily. Renewing the mind is facilitated when meditating on His word. Allow His word to bring comfort to you as you are led into your new season. I encourage you not to bring the remnants of the old season into the new one God has brought forth. It would be like a snow storm occurring in the middle of a July summer day. The old cannot mix with the new. The joy He provides cannot be taken by any thing and/or any one.

Prayer:

Lord, I come before you and I bless your Holy name. I ask that you provide me with the wisdom I need to detach from my current season as you prepare me for my new. Lord may you equip me as you bring the joy that only you can provide. In the Mighty name of Jesus, Amen.

Declaration:

____

____

____

____

____

____

____

> For you created my inmost being; you knit me together in my mother's womb. I praise you because I am fearfully and wonderfully made; your works are wonderful, I know that full well.
>
> *Psalm 139:13-14 (NIV)*

One of the tactics of the enemy is to make us feel as if we are not enough. Not enough to be a mom, not enough to be the great employee, not enough to accomplish greatness in life. In spite of that, God says otherwise. When He created us, He created something good, long-lasting, and God doesn't make mistakes. Whenever your mind gets clouded with thoughts that are contrary to what or who God says you are, pick up His word. The Bible is the truth and for every dart the enemy tries to throw your way or discourage you with, there is a word that repels it. Declare today that the battle in your mind is won by the power of Christ that lives in you. May His peace shine upon you as you adjust your crown and continue to press forward.

Personal prayer:

Declaration:

Day 71

As single mothers our days can sometimes, if not at all times, feel like a heavy load; a load that oftentimes we have to physically carry alone. Whether it be the groceries, laundry, or a day full of things to do and repeating yourself to the children, it's a burdensome weight to carry. Understand that God does not want us to carry this heavy load on our own. Matthew 11:28-30 (NKJV) reminds us of the ease we have navigating through life when we allow God to take over. Proverbs 31:17 (NKJV) speaks of the virtuous woman "...girding herself with strength" (NKJV). To gird means to prepare (Merriam Webster dictionary). What does preparing yourself for the day look like? Today, I encourage you to take a moment with God and lay out all of the things that are causing your load to be heavy at His feet. Give Him time to respond as His response will be the very thing you need to strengthen you in this season.

Prayer:

Today I pray Isaiah 40:31 over you, she who hopes in the Lord will renew her strength. She will soar on wings like eagles; she will run and not grow weary, she will walk and not be faint. In Jesus name Amen.

Declaration:

____

____

____

____

____

____

____

____

____

Day 72

Being joyful is a choice we make in life. It's something that we receive from God. He desires for us to have joy despite the seasons we encounter in life. God created us to be content in all seasons as life is not always going to be one smooth sailing. Psalm 46:1-3 (NKJV) is a great testament to what we deal with in life at times. It also reminds us of how God is, "A very present help in trouble" (v.1). The word "present" indicates that God is there during every trial we face despite how nasty it may seem. Because of His presence, while in the matter, it will pass: It is what is required of us to have joy and be joyful (James 1:2, NKJV). Choosing to be joyful is obedience. If we walk around downtrodden like the world while suffering hardships, how is God's light going to be seen?

Personal prayer:

Declaration:

____

____

____

____

____

____

____

____

____

> But seek first the kingdom of God and his righteousness, and all these things shall be added to you.
>
> *Matthew 6:33 (NKJV)*

Loneliness is a chore. A chore is defined as, "An unpleasant but necessary task" (Oxford languages). In single parenting, loneliness is a feeling that creeps up from time to time. Although it can bring discomfort, loneliness is sometimes needed in order for God's will to be completed in our lives. The verse above reminds us of this fact. It is in this season of loneliness where we find God; distractions are inexistent. Once we conquer this feeling, we will have the tools to help our children when they experience their season of loneliness. In Joshua 1:9 (NKJV), God commands us to be "...strong and of good courage." because He is always with us. As a command given, we need to take action and obey. On this day, I encourage you to pray Joshua 1:9 (NKJV) over your life.

Personal prayer:

Declaration:

____

____

____

____

____

____

____

____

____

Day 74

There is power in the words that we speak. Consequently, it is why we need to be careful with what we say to our children as well as how we speak in moments of agitation. The verse above highlights how our words have the power to dictate how we feel, which in turn would dictate our circumstance. What are you proclaiming? If we walk around claiming how tired we are about a situation, we would just get worn down by it as opposed to asking God what He wants us to learn or understand while in the situation.

Personal prayer:

Declaration:

Day 75

> Again he said to me, "prophesy to these bones, and say to them, 'O dry bones hear the word of the Lord!"
>
> *Ezekiel 37:4 (NKJV)*

There are seasons in life when we experience droughts in our lives. These droughts can look like everything is going wrong all at once. The children are going haywire, work is getting stressful, life seems to be in a state of chaos. These are the moments in which we turn to God like never before. Like the good Father that He is, He always has a resolve for us. God's part is providing the solutions. Our part, after seeking help from God, is to obey. This can be done by responding to tough situations with what God has given us to use. Today I ask you, what are you speaking to your dry places? Are you speaking from your own strength and frustration? Or are you utilizing God's word to decree His will over the dry bones in your life?

Personal prayer:

Declaration:

____

____

____

____

____

____

____

____

____

Day 76

As women, sometimes we let our emotions get the best of us which can lead to making impulsive decisions. This can be a dangerous place to be as a single mom. With all that is required of us and from us on a daily basis, we cannot afford to live based on the first things we feel. Doing so may cause harm to our children and leave a lasting impact. For example, when saying something out of anger that would affect their self esteem, consequently, would lead them down a life path lacking confidence and/or believing in themselves. The key to not living or making decisions based on the rashness of emotions is to remain in God; to dwell there. If we stay in God's word, His word will abide in us, teach us, correct us, and nurture us so that we live and respond to life in a fruitful way. Today, I encourage you to remain in God because nothing is possible without Him.

Prayer:

Lord, I come before you laying it all down at your feet. My anger, frustration, sadness, and whatever other emotion I am feeling on this day. Lord, I will look to you, no longer will I look at anything else but you father. I put on confidence, I will live in the spirit by remaining in you. No longer will I live emotionally.
In Jesus name Amen.

Declaration:

____

____

____

____

____

____

____

Day 77

> And Jesus answered and said to her, "Martha, Martha, you are worried and troubled about many things. But one thing is needed, and Mary has chosen that good part, which will not be taken away from her."
>
> *Luke 10:41-42 (NKJV)*

There are moments during this season of single parenting in which we can run ourselves dry. We keep going, going, and going by putting everyone else's needs at the forefront. Doing so can leave our cups empty, leaving us with nothing left to give. Pouring from an empty cup can have many side effects attached to it, one being irritability. Have you ever had a moment or day where any little thing bothered you or ticked you off? If so, you, my friend, we're pouring from an empty cup. This irritability is a sign that we need to get back to Jesus' feet. As we see in the story above, Martha was busy being irritated with Mary's choice to remain at Jesus's feet. Yet, Jesus corrected her letting her know that being at his feet is all she needs. We need to be like Mary and remain at Jesus' feet to receive the food we need to get through life and its demands.

Personal prayer:

Declaration:

> Those who plant in tears will harvest with shouts of joy. They weep as they go to plant their seed but they sing as they return with harvest.
>
> *Psalm 126:5-6 (NLT)*

Tears are shed for many reasons. People cry when they are hurt, sad, mad, or happy. Despite the circumstances causing the flow of tears, a common effect of crying is relief. There is a sense of comfort that is felt after crying. In single parenting, there are many tears that are shed. Know that the tears being released are not done so in vain. As the verse above expresses, there is a return on these tears that are being shed. That return is joy; something that only God can give. Today, I encourage you to remember that God has not forgotten you. He sees every tear you have shed. He wants you to know that He is with you as you continue to remain in Him. His strength will bring you the joy you have been longing for.

Prayer:

Lord, I come before you, thanking you for your word says you will never leave me nor forsake me. I pray that as you wipe these tears with your mighty hand, I can feel your joy in the morning. In Jesus name Amen.

Declaration:

Day 79

There are many battles we face in life: in our minds, with the other parent, with our children, or at work. One thing we need to remember is that despite how difficult or annoying the battle is, there is no need to feel or act defeated. This is because God is in our corner. When we have God on our side, we have authority. Just as Jesus reminded the disciples of the authority He gave them, as His daughters, we also have authority over the battles we face. This allows us to not be defeated or overwhelmed by the weight of the fight because God's power is greater than anything we face. I encourage you to remember that this authority is only evident as long as God is in your corner. This requires a level of grace and grace requires humility. When using the authority given by God, remember to use it gracefully.

Prayer:

Lord, I come before you thanking you for the authority I have as your daughter. I pray for the wisdom I need to use this authority with grace, the same grace you give to me. Create in me a clean heart that I may be wise with the authority you have entrusted in me. In Jesus name Amen.

Declaration:

____

____

____

____

____

____

____

Day 80

iving a life of gratitude requires living a life of service. Jesus showed His disciples the meaning of serving; He served by teaching, healing others, equipping the disciples, even His crucifixion was a way to serve the world. Sometimes "life happens" and may cause someone to not want to serve. For example, before being captive and executed, Jesus asked God to take the situation away if it was in His will (Luke 22:42, NKJV). Next, (v. 43) we see that He was strengthened by an angel from heaven. Just as Jesus needed to be strengthened, we as single moms need to be strengthened on a daily basis. Rearing our children and making sure we raise decent human beings is how we serve. Today, let's remember to serve with a thankful heart even if the kids are raising havoc. Remember that God's love and faithfulness provides the strength we need to keep going. If He did it for Jesus, He will definitely do it for us.

Personal prayer:

Declaration:

____

____

____

____

____

____

____

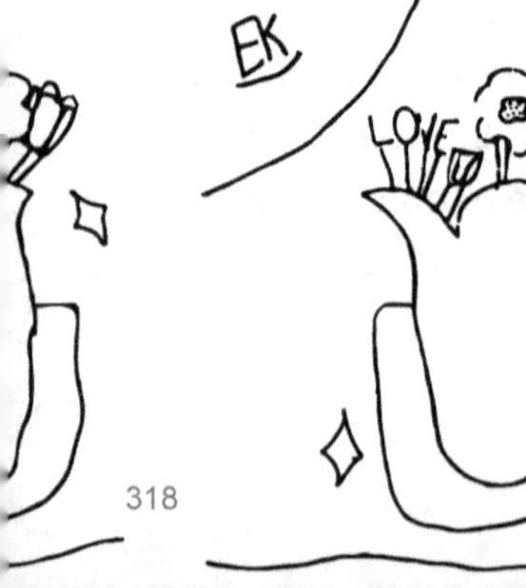

EK
LOVE

EK
LOVE

> I and the children the LORD
> has given me serve as signs and
> warnings to Israel from the LORD
> of Heaven's Armies who dwells in his
> Temple on Mount zion.
>
> *Isaiah 8:18 (NLT)*

Children are gifts from God. He trusts us with such gifts because He knows we are capable of handling the gifts well. Children are not only gifts but they are also signs of God's will for our lives; the indication of God's will being evident and transcending through our bloodlines for generations. When one has a child, a legacy is created. God's will is not only effective for us but also for our children. Today, I encourage you to remember this fact, the child you see walking around the house, the child that may be working your last nerve, is a gift and a sign of God's will in your life and for the upcoming generations. Remember to continue to partner with God through this season. As you keep Him as the foundation and center of your life, your home, your bloodline, your legacy, and the generations to come will be blessed.

Personal prayer:

Declaration:

____

____

____

____

____

____

____

____

____

____

Day 82

When we first find out we are expecting, one thing we do, or rather, the first thing we do is pray and ask God for a healthy baby. This is the first indication of the fiery motherly instinct we, as women, have within. This instinct needs to continue throughout parenting despite the circumstances that occur. There are times in parenting where we may start to question ourselves on whether we are doing a good job. This can happen especially in single parenting because we are doing it, physically, alone. Remember that the gift God gave you is a testament that He trusts you. If you have been wondering whether you are doing well in parenting, take a minute and look back. Reflect on those moments you thought were going to take you out. Think about how God's hand has been with you since the beginning.; as His hand is on you, His Spirit dwells within you. You are capable despite how hard it is or despite the actions of your child. You are a phenomenal mother as you continue to partner with God in this season.

Personal prayer:

Declaration:

Day 83

Paul was speaking to Timothy, his mentee, and like a son to him. Paul was reminding and encouraging Timothy to remember what he has learned: The truth, God's truth. As Timothy would continue with his life assignment of teaching God's word, His spirit would forever be within Timothy, leading him through the ups and downs of life. Today, I encourage you as Paul encouraged Timothy to not give in to society's ways of child rearing. There are so many distractions that are darts of the enemy aiming to distort the light and ways of God. Remember God has given you the blueprint for child rearing through the Holy Spirit. I pray that you can be sensitive to the Holy Spirit and heed His still soft voice in this journey.

Personal prayer:

Declaration

Day 84

God is a mighty God that has many names. Although He has many names, He is still the same God. Calling on Him using a specific name unlocks the door to the situation being faced. In single parenting we face different situations. As a result, there will be times when we need to call on the appropriate name for our situation in order to see God's manifestation. Yes, God hears and answers all prayers but just like there are different doctors to care for the different parts and needs of our body, knowing the exact name to call delivers a direct response. Here is a list of names I've learned about so far in my journey, I pray you are encouraged to use one in your time of need.

Jehovah Tsaba (Sa-Buh): The God who fights for me.
Jehovah Shalom: The God of peace.
Jehovah Rapha: The God who heals.
Jehovah Jireh: The God that provides.
El Roi: The God that sees me.
El Olam: Everlasting God.
Adonai: The God over all.

Personal prayer:

Declaration:

____

____

____

____

____

____

____

> "I pray that God, the source of hope,
> will fill you completely with joy and peace
> because you trust Him. Then you will
> overflow with confident hope through
> the power of the Holy Spirit."
>
> Romans 15:13 (NLT)

In this single parenting journey, there are times when we receive words that are promises from God. These promises can be about anything we've prayed for, such as a new car, job, a husband, or something we did not pray for but God promised it anyway. Time goes by and yet the promises have not manifested. These moments can make one start to doubt or lose hope over what was spoken over your life. When these moments occur, especially during the holiday season or when we see that promise happening for someone else, we need to give it to God and get into His word. During these seasons of feeling "hopeless" about the promises you are waiting for from God, I encourage you to read a story in the Bible about someone's hope being restored. God is not a man that He should lie. Remember that His promises are yes and amen (2 Corinthians 1:20, NKJV). Go to the source from where your hope comes from and allow God to refill you.

Personal prayer:

Declaration:

____

____

____

____

____

____

____

> You have need of endurance, so that
> when you have done the will of God,
> you may receive what was promised.
>
> Hebrews 10:36 (ESV)

This is a reminder that endurance is essential in life. It is defined as getting through a trial without compromising or wavering (www.fccmacon.com). There will be times where God will have us in between seasons; we can be between a hard place and a promise. It is imperative that we endure and run a good race. Let's look at this scenario from a sports perspective. When a team is in the finals, they have to play against other teams in order to get a championship. This season requires a team to play against other teams several times, with the team who wins the most out of seven games taking the championship. Think about the endurance the players must have in order to keep facing the same opponents in order to get a victory. I imagine how the players must train more than ever during finals to keep their endurance. The life of a single parent is no different, there will be times where we face the same battles continually. Let's remember where to go in order to strengthen the endurance we need in order to receive our promise.

Personal prayer:

Declaration:

____

____

____

____

____

____

____

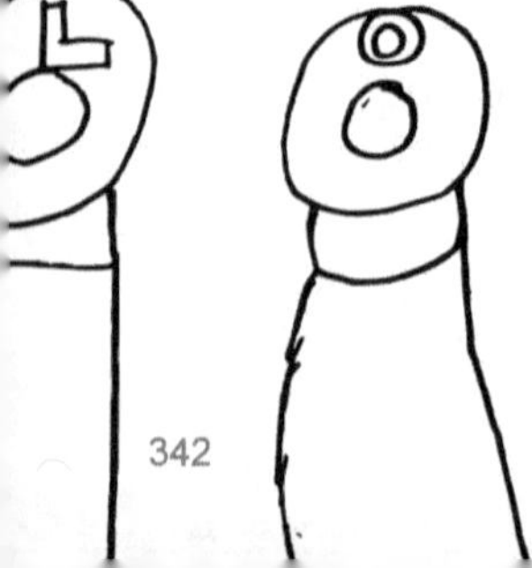

Day 87

Parenting single but not alone (with God) requires a distinction compared to parenting single alone (without God). Those outside looking in, they should be able to see this distinction. This can be evident if we live our lives filled with faith. Hebrews 12:1 states the need to get rid of the burden that would cause our faith to waiver (NLT). Sometimes as single mothers, we can have a tendency to try and do everything on our own and not ask for help. This mindset can be a deterrent because we get boggled down when we are on overload. Once the Holy Spirit dwells in us, He directs us to see how certain people in our lives can help with the weight distribution. Think of it as a relay race. The runners run a certain amount of miles before they pass the baton to the next runner. It's a team effort so that the runner does not take on the sole responsibility of winning the entire race. This is how God desires for us to live our lives. John 14:16-18 (NLT) is a reminder of this truth. I encourage you to be sensitive to the Holy Spirit in this single mommy season and remember to pass the baton when needed.

Personal prayer:

Declaration:

____

____

____

____

____

____

____

Day 88

As single mothers, we are the leaders in our home. Leaders have influence and a huge impact on the lives of those who follow them; it's important to lead with integrity. Having integrity means to do the right thing even when no one is looking (https://www.indeed.com/career-advice/career-development/integrity-at-work). As believers and knowing God's omnipresence, we know that He is always looking. Although we are the leaders of our home, God is the head of our households. This is the only way we can live with integrity. We live our lives knowing that whatever we do will require an explanation to Him. Explanations are only needed when someone needs clarification of a vague action. Let's remember that we are the first leaders our children encounter. Be encouraged that as we continue to allow God to be the head of our lives and homes, we will continue to be blessed and it will trickle down from generation to generation.

Prayer:

Lord, I come before you and I submit myself to you. I know that parenting a child in the way you would have me exceeds my human capability. I need your assistance. In Jesus name amen.

Declaration:

____

____

____

____

____

____

____

____

____

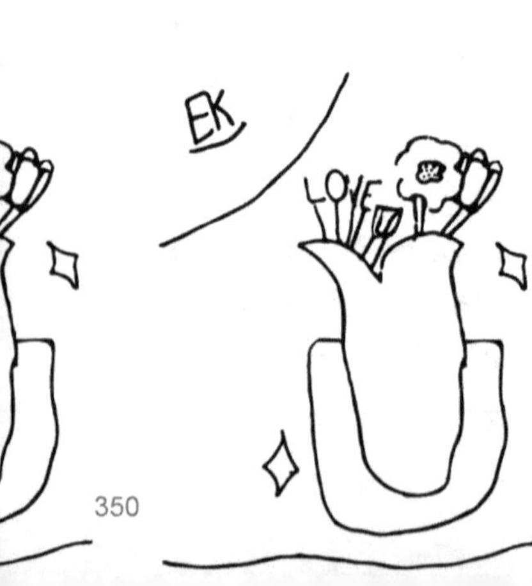

Day 89

> For God is not the author of
> confusion but of peace, as in all
> the churches of the saints.
>
> *1 Corinthians 14:33 (NKJV)*

There are days when life can shift us off balance. Sometimes, things commence to fall apart before the day even starts; like having to fuss with the children to get up and get ready for school. Maybe the morning began great but then things took a left turn at work. Despite the circumstance that occurred to cause the sudden change, God does not expect us to stay unbalanced. God's intention is for us to have sound minds and live in peace. Here is a quote by Bishop T.D. Jakes, "God's word will accomplish what it is sent out to do. He says, "I will not give up on you. I will keep hammering until you are balanced in your thinking and whole in your judgements" (Woman Thou Art Loosed Bible). This quote reminds us of God's thoughts towards His children. If God is not willing to give up on us, then we must continue pushing on our end as well. Think of it as giving birth. Before a birthing mom has to push she feels the pressure. The pushing coupled with the pressure produces the baby entering the world. As God applies the pressure on His end, we need to push on our end. The result, our victory of a sound mind. Having a sound mind will help us navigate through life better. Things will change but we will remain grounded in Him.

Personal prayer:

Declaration:

Day 90

There can be moments in this single-mother season where we can feel like we got the short end of the stick. At Least, that's how it can feel when you are the custodial parent; causing one to work their schedule around their childrens'. There are many tasks to accomplish in what seems like very little time. Today, I want to encourage you by sharing that instead of looking at this season as a "short-end-of-the-stick-season", think of it as a training season! See it from a perspective of God cultivating you for your Proverbs 31 woman season. The tasks we accomplish as single mothers will be an addition to our next season. When we read about the Proverbs 31 woman (Proverbs 31:10-31, NKJV) we read about her character, attributes, and success in everything she does for her family and home. Each and everyone of us have these characteristics we excel in (even if you feel like you don't, you sis, are doing your thing!) and guess what, we are excelling physically alone! So, imagine the growth we will experience during our wife season! I pray that today you are encouraged and remember that this season is one in which you have the advantage. Trust the process and enjoy the training season. I leave you with this quote written by Bishop T.D. Jakes as a declaration over your lives:

"You are a modern woman. You are free to be everything God has gifted you to be. Do not allow the world to define what your womanhood should be. Know God's call to your life and obey it. There has never been a time when women have been more free. So explore, express, and enjoy the opportunities He sets before you" (Woman Thou Art Loosed Bible).

THE AUTHOR

My name is Georgianna Martinez, I was born and raised in the Bronx, New York and currently, while writing to you, residing in Westchester, NY. I am the youngest of four girls and was raised in a single-parent household from the age of 9, which is when my dad left the family. I have a beautiful, caring, loving, and funny 9-year-old daughter named Evanna. I'm an aunt to five nieces and one nephew, whom I had the pleasure of helping to raise. By profession, I'm a Special Education teacher in New York City and I currently teach 5th-grade math. During my "downtime", I love to read, watch movies, and spend time with my family. I love to travel and create memories with my daughter. Above all of the things I've mentioned about myself, I must humbly mention that I am a lover of Christ. It is through this love that my passion for helping others, especially single moms, ignites. I pray that as He instructed me and guided me in writing this devotional, your life will be BLESSED!

blogsite: www.mommysaccess.com

Instagram: amommysaccess_withgod

About
THE AUTHOR'S DAUGHTER/ILLUSTRATOR

My name is Evanna. I love to eat cakes, going to the Olive Garden and other outdoor foods like Burger King, Wendy's, and Popeyes. I love playing basketball and I love to draw. Drawing helps me stay calm and brings me peace. I love to travel with my mom and our other family members. Lastly, I love to learn about God and worship by singing and listening to Christian rap music.

www.ingramcontent.com/pod-product-compliance
Lightning Source LLC
Chambersburg PA
CBHW050315160726
48002CB00001B/39